Shadow of a Drought

A Photo Essay — St. Martin 2015

Postcard from the Future

The climate is influenced by many factors and is notoriously difficult to model. Temperatures are increasing, and weather patterns are likely to change as well. The frequency of extreme conditions—from storms to droughts—is also forecast to increase. Most models predict that our area, already dry, will receive even less rainfall in the coming decades.

Feast Before the Famine

These Snowy Egrets—and many other wetland foragers—are quick to take advantage of small prey trapped in disappearing ponds. Small ponds carved from the edges of larger ones by roads and other development often evaporate completely during drought. Birds congregate for a few days of easy hunting, but then must move on when the ponds vanish.

Last Refuges

The ponds that remain stand out against the parched hillsides. They are alive with the buzz of insects and the chatter of birds. Green leaves reflect in the surface of the water, defying the sun.

Danger Begins at Home

Dying mangroves drove a large egret colony to nest in a new location beside a pond that dried into nothing. Exposed on all sides, young egrets were more vulnerable to predators and quick to leave their nests in fright. Bodies of fallen chicks rest beneath the mangroves.

Dying Young

Adult birds can move from pond to pond when conditions become inhospitable. Until they are able to fly, chicks are not always so lucky. A prime nesting spot in February can become a deadly mistake by April, but by then it is too late. Between extreme rains that could flood a nest and drought that can parch a pond, Black-necked Stilts and other breeding pond birds walk a fine line every year.

Tapestry of Survival

On scrubby hillsides, each color reflects a strategy for dealing with dry weather. Some trees and shrubs lose their leaves altogether to conserve moisture, leaving bare branches in white, brown and red. Yellows, oranges and greens are showcased by others, preparing to lose leaves or starting to grow new ones in hopeful anticipation of rain.

Hungry Beasts

The plight of livestock during the drought has been impossible to ignore. Lack of food has brought them down from the hills and through fences, onto roadways and into gardens in search of anything green to eat. Some relief has come in the form of hay and animal feed. In a future that looks increasingly dry, do livestock have a place on St. Martin?

Hills on Fire

Brushfires are common during the spring dry season. Whipped by the easterly wind, they can burn dry grass fast enough to leave trees untouched. Insects fly from the flames into the waiting mouths of Cattle Egrets. In an average year, burned patches explode into green with the next rainfall. Without the rain, barren hillsides wait.

Turned to Stone

Hillsides cleared for sugarcane plantations lost their soil, with no native roots left to hold it in place. Tenacious plants and grasses maintain an illusion of fertility as long as they can before finally revealing a legacy of stone.

The Colors of Drought

As the days and weeks march on, the shorelines of our ponds are redrawn, each time a bit smaller. Their colors change, too. Receding waters darken into shades of tan and dusky orange. Salt concentrates lethally in the diminishing liquid. As evaporating salt ponds become hypersaline, Halobacteria bring a bright pink color to waters where nothing else can survive.

The Pattern Maker

Glorious and chaotic natural landscapes are transformed into oddly lifeless patterns: a cracked web of dried mud, a hillside mosaic of bare stones, a cluster of bare branches reaching hopefully towards the sky.

Like a Mirage

Mudflats stretch across empty basins, creased and cracked, crisscrossed by tracks. In the distance, the reflection of the sun glints off pools of water. Heat rises from the evaporating surface like a mirage.

Ghosts in the Mud

If you've ever wondered what animals live beneath the murky surface of our ponds, a drought is certainly one way to find out. Fish, crabs, snails and other aquatic animals dot the advancing mudflats. They often rest perfectly preserved, as if they had been mummified by the sun before scavengers came upon them.

History Exposed

Receding waters reveal hidden structures in the Great Salt Pond. The stone walls dividing salt pans mirror the slave walls partitioning the hills. Once the economic and cultural heart of the island, the Great Salt Pond has diminished in recent decades—both literally and figuratively—but still offers a connection to the history and heritage of St. Martin.

Shame Surfaces

Out of sight, out of mind, but dumping trash in a pond never made it go away. Drought reveals some of our worst attributes: laziness, ignorance and a lack of respect for the environment that sustains us. It tells the story of material consumption that outstrips our ability and will to manage our waste, particularly under the inherent constraints of living on the most densely populated island in the Caribbean.

Vintage Cars

How many cars have been dumped into our ponds? A ring of rusted bodies circles Chevrise during the dry season. A water truck crumbles in the mangroves. The drought revealed this carcass in a pond barely bigger than car itself.

A Different Kind of River

It's not quite a river, and it's not exactly water, but a Muscovy Duck and her ducklings waddle through it anyway. What could be mistaken for the last muddy pool in a drying pond is actually waste water flowing in from a nearby apartment building. Pollution that might normally trickle into ponds unnoticed sticks out like a sore thumb when it's the only water there is.

Nowhere to Hide

The drought magnifies our misdeeds. Dirty oil twists, joins and splits in liquid patterns on the surface of stagnant water. There is an illusion that what we dump can be absorbed, but that illusion dissolves when our pollution doesn't.

Gray Skies

What curse kept gray skies from releasing rain day in and day out? El Niño? Dust from the Sahara? Some disaster of our own creation that we may not understand for years to come?

Deep Roots

Long ago—before tourism, before sugarcane, before humans—the island was covered in native vegetation. The hillsides were carpeted with the trees and plants that were hardy enough to withstand storm and drought. The spots of green and spaces between show us how rare these deep roots are today.

Bare Branches

In the Caribbean, many trees lose their leaves to conserve water in the dry season. As the months drag on, barren trees abound, from hillside to roadside. They stand, somewhere between living and dead, bare branches reaching towards the sky.

Salty Water

Drought strains the very concept of what is natural. Naturally-occurring microbes turn water pink when the concentration of salt rises enough—a phenomenon familiar enough to those who remember the days of salt production. Knowing it is natural doesn't make it feel normal.

Still Life

There are so many ways to die in a drought—not enough water, not enough food, not enough oxygen, too much salt. Giant Land Crabs have the tools of survivors. They are equally adept at extracting oxygen from air or water and can retire to their sealed burrows for months. Even so, the extreme conditions were enough to stop them in their tracks.

The Crab Cycle

Known in French as the Crabier—crab eater—this Yellow-crowned Night Heron returns the favor, providing sustenance to fiddler crabs near the water's edge. Although this is an ancient cycle, at least three of these herons were found dead in the same small area this summer. Receding waters may have left them with less prey—one was seen trying to eat an unrecognizable, rotting mass—driving them to famine or sickness.

No Place Left to Grow
A web of barren mangrove branches looks like the Halloween version of a wetland. In the background, flecks of green grass are finally showing on the stone-covered hillside that had been bare for months after a brush fire swept through.

Magical Colors

The strange alchemy of life meets the strange alchemy of humankind. A light rain has brought an explosion of green to the surface of a pond, but who knows what nutrients have supercharged these algae or what proteins have been whipped into a meringue by the wind.

Beginning Again

With each rain signaling the hope of fertile times ahead, the hills begin transitioning into green again. Leaf by leaf and flower by flower, each tree and plant interprets the weather according to its own biology. Meanwhile, the forecast remains ominous, but far from certain. Only time will tell.

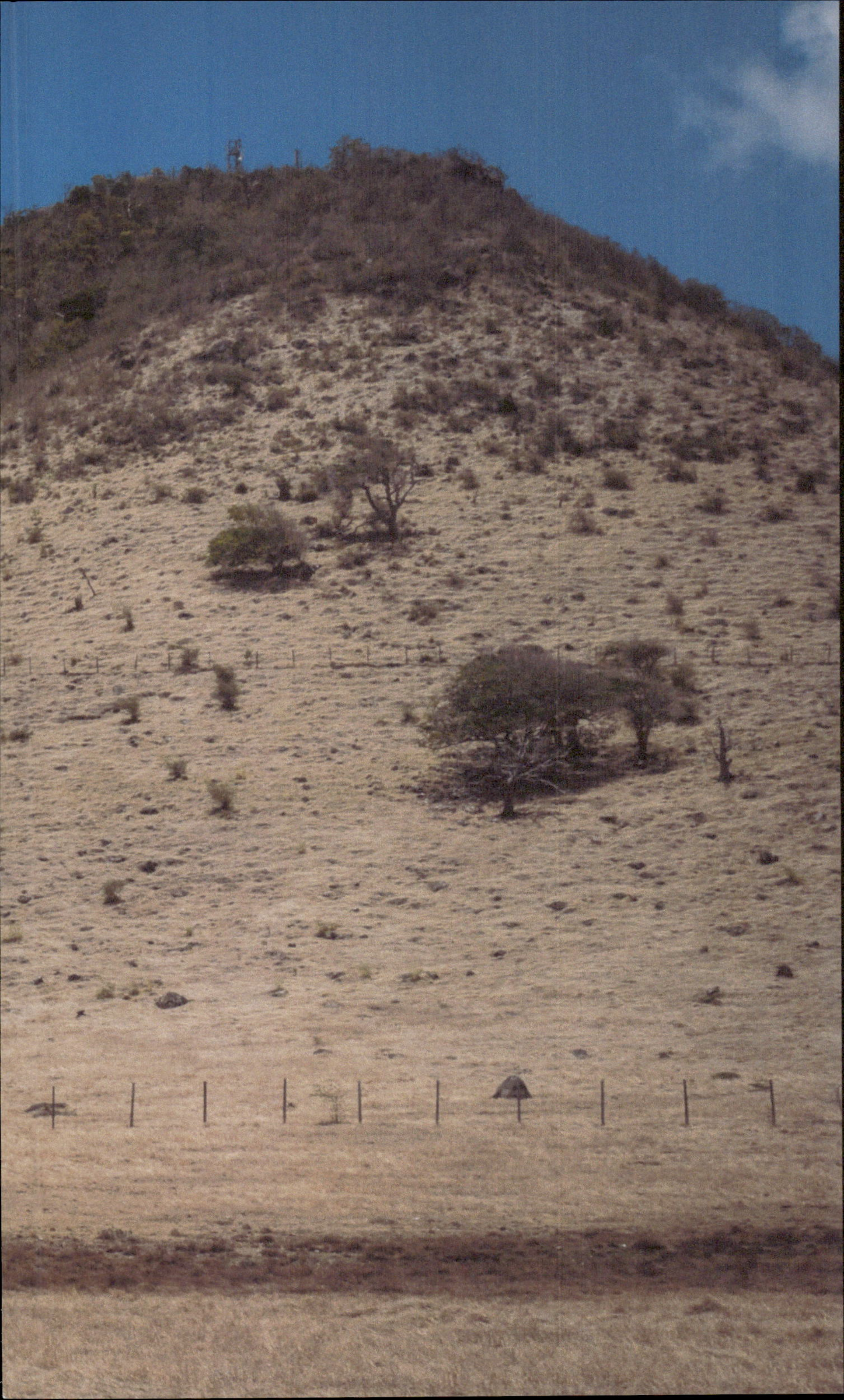

Shadow of a Drought was produced by Les Fruits de Mer as a companion piece to the 2015 Migratory Bird Festival. All photos and text by Mark Yokoyama.

Les Fruits de Mer is a non-profit association based in St. Martin whose core mission is to raise awareness about local nature, culture, and history. The organization carries out this mission through publications, an education program, and special public outreach events that entertain, inspire, and inform. For more information, and to join, visit lesfruitsdemer.com.